Garden Hacks

70 SMART, SUSTAINABLE TIPS FOR GARDENERS

Garden Hacks

Filip Johansson

murdoch books

London | Sydney

Preface

Many of us are drawn to all that grows and dream of a lush, beautiful garden. Perhaps we imagine ourselves eating a sun-ripened tomato in our very own greenhouse. But then reality catches up with us and we think it must be difficult, expensive and lots of hard work. I'm here to tell you, it doesn't have to be!

I grew up with a small garden and have lived most of my life in an apartment, but a few years ago I moved to a small homestead in southern Sweden. That's when gardening completely took over my life. I've had an allotment for quite some time and wasn't a complete novice when it came to gardening, but it's only in the last five years that I've really given it a go and learned most of what I know about caring for a garden. Someone said I was 'handy', but I don't believe in that concept. For me, being handy is about finding the courage to try. Those who dare, grow handy pretty quickly!

Being able to grow food to sustain ourselves and to build and fix tools and other necessities boosts our self-confidence and makes us feel proud. It's a great feeling. In this book, I hope to convey it to you. For the past few years, I've been sharing garden hacks as well as other tips and tricks on social media, and now I'm gathering the best ones here! Someone suggested that I write a 'bathroom book of gardening' and while that may not be entirely off the mark, I think I'm aiming just a little higher ...

This book is meant to inspire you to take shortcuts and find ingenious solutions to the various challenges you may encounter in your garden. You might think that gardening is only a spring and summer hobby, but your garden is alive all year round and there is always something fun to busy yourself with. Therefore, the projects in this book have been organised by season, so that you can find useful ideas and things to do regardless of when you dive in. Gardening is not that hard and you already have most of the things you need to succeed! So go out there, let go of your performance anxiety and get started!

Have fun and good luck!
Filip Johansson, Lunnarp, Sweden

Spring

This time of year, as your garden begins to come alive again, you may feel those green fingers starting to itch. Perhaps you have already started propagating indoors and can't wait to transplant your seedlings into the ground, or maybe you are all about direct seeding. I – and many like me – usually sow way too many seeds, but I can't stop myself from buying even more. It's all about finding fun and clever tricks to make sure you succeed with everything you sow.

Before getting started, you need to make sure that the most crucial part of your garden – the soil – is prepped and ready. When you sow or transplant your precious little seedlings, it's important to give them the best possible conditions, which can be summarised as: water, nutrients and protection. Once your garden takes off things can happen very quickly, and your plants may need a little help to stay healthy and not be damaged by the wind. The solution is various supports and climbing frames. And remember, all those seeds you bought could grow into a great gift later in the spring or summer!

14   Spring

Seed Bombs

→ Scatter seeds with soil to grow in, and let the sun and rain take care of the planting. To succeed, the soil must be loamy – and there is a simple test to determine if it's up to scratch. Try rolling some soil between your fingers until it's about as thick as a pencil. If it holds together, it contains the right amount of clay. Otherwise you can buy clay powder and mix it in. Playing in the muck to increase biodiversity is the perfect Sunday pastime!

YOU WILL NEED

→ clay-rich soil (if the soil in your garden is a bit too sandy, you can mix in shop-bought clay powder until it passes the test described above – equal amounts of clay and soil usually works well)
→ bucket
→ a little water to moisten the soil so that you can shape it into balls
→ flower seeds (choose native species, preferably native wildflowers)

STEP BY STEP

1. Pour clay-rich soil into a bucket and add some water.
2. Mix in the seeds.
3. Work it into a paste with your hands.
4. Shape the paste into little golf balls and squeeze out all the water with your hands.
5. Leave the balls in a protected place and let them dry in the sun.
6. Throw the seed bombs in a spot that could use some flowers and let the sun and rain do the rest.

Homemade Seed-starting Soil

→ When sowing, you'll want to use soil that drains well and is nutrient-poor. Too many nutrients can damage tiny new roots as the salts cause the roots to 'burn' and become unable to absorb water and nutrients. And soil that is too moist can lead to fungal disease. But you don't need to buy a specific seed-starting mix; it's super easy to make your own by mixing sand, regular soil and cheap garden soil (i.e. peat moss)! This also helps to minimise the use of peat moss, which isn't great in terms of its impact on the environment and the climate. In order to make my seed-starting soil fluffy and remove any big clumps, I use a bicycle basket to sift the soil and the peat moss.

YOU WILL NEED

→ 2 parts sand
→ seed tray or pot
→ bicycle basket
→ 1 part soil dug up from your garden
→ 1 part cheap garden soil or peat moss

STEP BY STEP

1. Pour the sand into your seed tray or pot.
2. Using the bicycle basket, sift the regular soil into the tray or pot.
3. Sift the cheap garden soil through the bicycle basket in the same way.
4. Mix well.
5. Sterilise your soil (see page 19).

Spring

Quick Trick to Sterilise Seed-starting Soil

→ Seed-starting soil – both shop-bought and homemade – can contain bacteria, fungi and fungus gnat eggs, and it would be a shame to have your tiny, delicate seeds damaged or outcompeted. To increase their capacity to germinate, it's a good idea to sterilise the soil. There are a few different ways, but my favourites are either baking the soil or pouring boiling water over it. The water method is particularly useful if you don't need to sterilise big quantities. Whichever method you choose, I recommend being outside. This is because soil that is heated develops a strong odour.

YOU WILL NEED

BAKING METHOD:
→ barbecue
→ baking tray

WATER METHOD:
→ water
→ kettle or saucepan

STEP BY STEP

BAKING METHOD:
1. Fire up the barbecue.
2. Fill the baking tray with soil. Place the baking tray on the hot barbecue and leave for 10–20 minutes. It should start to smoke.
3. Allow the soil to cool before sowing seeds.

WATER METHOD:
1. Boil the water in a kettle or saucepan.
2. Pour the boiling water over the seed-starting soil.
3. Allow the soil to cool before sowing seeds.

Keep Your Seeds Moist Using Cardboard

→ A trick I use for keeping seeds moist is to cover them with a piece of cardboard. It prevents rapid evaporation but doesn't keep a tight seal, so the risk of mould is very low. Most seeds germinate within two weeks and, with the cardboard as protection, watering when you sow is usually sufficient. However, make sure to check after a week and add a little water if the soil seems too dry.

YOU WILL NEED

→ soil
→ seed tray
→ water
→ seeds
→ a piece of cardboard, large enough to cover your seeds

STEP BY STEP

1. Pour most of the soil into the seed tray and add water until it's completely soaked.
2. Sow your seeds.
3. Cover the seeds with more soil and lightly moisten the top layer.
4. Cover the seeds with the cardboard.
5. Remove the cardboard after one to two weeks, when the seeds have germinated and have begun to peek through the soil.

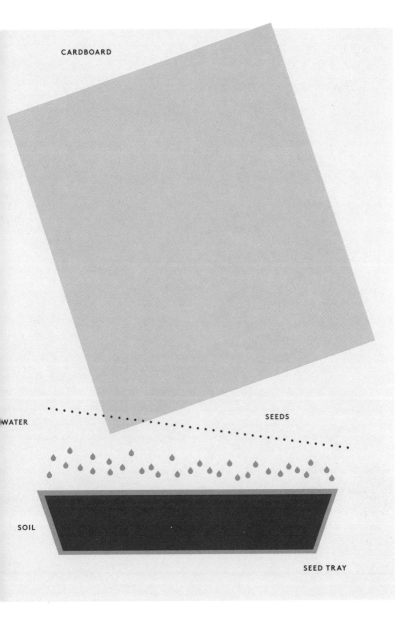

CARDBOARD

WATER

SEEDS

SOIL

SEED TRAY

Rapid Repotting

→ When propagating plants, you'll need to repot them – that is, replant them in a bigger pot as they grow – otherwise they will stop growing. The reason for not sowing directly into a bigger pot is partly that you don't want to take up too much space, and partly that a small seedling won't thrive in too much soil. If the soil mass becomes too big, wet and cold, the plant tends to grow poorly. Moderation is best! Here are some simple tricks to help you choose the right size pot and avoid getting soil all over your table and shoes.

YOU WILL NEED

→ a slightly bigger pot
→ large tub (optional)
→ soil

STEP BY STEP

1. To determine a good size for the pot you are replanting in, use your thumb to measure with. Place the pot with the plant into the bigger pot you plan to use. You should be able to fit at least one thumb's width between the edges of the old pot and the new.
2. Place everything inside a large tub if you like so any spilled soil can be collected.
3. Pour some soil into the bottom of the new pot. Place the old pot on the soil and adjust the amount of soil in the bottom of the new pot until the plant is at a good level.
4. Leave the old pot inside the new one and add soil around it.
5. Lift the plant out of the old pot and loosen up the roots.
6. Remove the old pot and place the plant in the hole that is left in the soil. Finally, sprinkle some soil on top.

Avoid Weeds in Your Garden Beds

→ The soil in your garden beds is guaranteed to contain weed seeds and if you're sowing directly in your beds you'll end up doing a lot of weeding. However, some newspaper and shop-bought soil can solve the problem! In many ways bought soil isn't great, but you only need a little – no more than a 40-litre (about 4 dry quarts) bag per bed. It has usually been heat treated to kill weed seeds and pests and, unfortunately, this also kills the good micro life – fungi, bacteria and worms – that's important for living, nutrient-rich soil. By only sprinkling over a little, you get the best of both worlds: a thin weed-free layer with rich soil underneath!

YOU WILL NEED

→ rake
→ newspaper
→ shop-bought garden soil
→ seeds
→ grass cuttings

STEP BY STEP

1. Prepare the garden bed by raking and clearing away any rocks and weeds.
2. Cover the entire surface with a layer or two of newspaper.
3. Spread a thin layer of shop-bought soil on top. The soil containing weed seeds has now been covered, which prevents sunlight from reaching it and the seeds from germinating.
4. Sow your seeds in the shop-bought soil.
5. Eventually, the newspaper will start to decompose. This usually happens when the plants have come up a bit. When this happens, cover the soil round the plants with grass cuttings. That way, no weeds will get through and you can still enjoy a weed-free garden bed!

Straight Seed Rows with a Sowing Plank or Cork Fork

→ Do you want straight rows of evenly spaced plants? Do you drink wine? Then I have the solution! Save all the wine corks and make a sowing plank or cork fork. It's smart and super simple!

YOU WILL NEED

SOWING PLANK:
- → pencil
- → a wooden plank, 1–2 metres (3¼–6½ feet) is a good length
- → 10–20 wine corks, depending on the desired spacing
- → screwdriver and 6 cm (2½ inch) long screws
- → a handle, e.g. from a kitchen drawer
- → rake

CORK FORK:
- → wine corks
- → pitchfork
- → rake

STEP BY STEP

SOWING PLANK:
1. Mark where on the plank you want to place the wine corks. The placement of the wine corks should correspond to the intended spacing of your plants (10 cm/ 4 inch is usually appropriate).
2. Attach a cork at each mark with a long screw, through the cork and down into the plank, making it stand out straight.
3. Screw a handle to the back of the plank to make it easy to manoeuvre.
4. Rake the seedbed before pressing the corks of the sowing plank into the soil to create perfectly spaced rows.

CORK FORK:
1. Press a cork onto each tine of the pitchfork.
2. Press the cork tines into your freshly raked garden bed to make little holes in which to sow or plant your seedlings.

Simple Way to Sow Tiny Seeds

→ If you have very tiny seeds, they can be difficult to sow with even spacing, and you may end up with clumps of plants here and there. Mix the seeds thoroughly with dry sand to make it easier, and to help you see where you have sown! Even better, use an old spice jar for sowing.

YOU WILL NEED

→ 1 part tiny seeds
→ a clean, empty spice jar
→ 50 parts sand

STEP BY STEP

1. Pour as many seeds as you want to sow into the jar.
2. Mix the seeds with about 50 times as much dry sand.
3. Shake the jar for at least 30 seconds to ensure that the contents are well mixed.
4. Sprinkle the mixture evenly into your seed row.

Rooting Pot

→ Cuttings can be taken in winter, spring or autumn and are a good way to propagate plants that you want more of or to give away. It's often quite easy, but sometimes cuttings can be a bit fussy. They like the soil to be moist deep down in the bottom of the pot and to be close to the edge of the pot for proper root development. An easy way to keep your cuttings happy, warm and moist enough is to use the pot-in-pot method. This provides more edges for the cuttings to press up against. And if you pour water into the small pot in the middle, the moisture reaches further down!

→ 1 part soil
→ 2 parts gravel
→ bucket
→ two pots that differ by at least 5 cm (2 inches) in diameter

STEP BY STEP

1. Cut or break off 10–15 cm (4–6 inches) long branches/stems from the plant you wish to propagate.
2. Remove almost all the leaves, except those at the very top.
3. Mix the soil and gravel in a bucket.
4. Fill the larger pot halfway with the gravel–soil mixture.
5. Place the smaller pot into the middle and fill up around it with the gravel–soil mixture. Don't pour any soil into the smaller pot.
6. Stick the cuttings into the soil between the edges of the two pots so that a third of each cutting sticks up above the surface.
7. Pour water into the small pot, making sure that the soil is kept moist but not too wet.

Spring

Temporary Mini Greenhouse

→ Once your cuttings or seedlings are planted, they may need protecting from strong sunlight and cold nights. Being replanted is stressful enough! Protect them during that initial time to give them a good start. All you need is a plastic bottle or container and a stick.

YOU WILL NEED

→ a clean, empty plastic bottle or container, e.g. for milk, juice, detergent or soap (those that are more white are fine, too)
→ knife
→ a stick with a side shoot

STEP BY STEP

1. Cut off the bottom of the bottle or container with the knife.
2. Place the bottle directly over the small plant.
3. Unscrew the cap to allow for some ventilation.
4. Lower the stick through the hole in the bottle so that the side shoot hooks over its mouth. This will prevent the bottle from blowing away.

Cardboard Weed Barrier

→ To give small propagated plants a good start once they have been transplanted to the garden bed, it's a good idea to cover the soil around them. This helps keep the soil moist and prevents competing weeds from growing. Usually, you would use organic material such as grass and leaves, but too much mulch creates a nice environment for slugs. A compromise is to cover only the area immediately surrounding the plant with a circle of cardboard, which provides many of the benefits of mulch but reduces the risk of a slug infestation.

YOU WILL NEED

→ scissors
→ a piece of cardboard, at least 30 × 30 cm (12 × 12 inches)

STEP BY STEP

1. Cut a circle of cardboard with a radius of about 15 cm (6 inches).
2. Make a straight cut into the centre of the circle.
3. At the centre, cut a hole with a 1–2 cm (½–¾ inch) radius.
4. Separate the edges of the cardboard at the cut and carefully place the circle around the plant so the stem sticks up through the small hole.

Water Roots with a Drink Carton

→ To make sure that the water reaches the bottom and to reduce evaporation from the surface, make some holes in a drink carton and bury it in the soil, then water through that. This way, the water ends up where it's most needed!

YOU WILL NEED
→ awl
→ a drink carton or equivalent with a screw cap
→ spade

STEP BY STEP

1. Using the awl, make some holes near the bottom on one side of the drink carton.
2. Bury the carton with the holes facing the plant. Leave only the top of the carton sticking up.
3. Fill the carton with water. Put the cap on to prevent debris or small insects from falling in.

Boost Biodiversity

→ A meadow can contain up to 50 species of flowers and other plants per square metre (11 square feet) – as many as in the rainforest! Creating and nurturing meadows is a great way to help boost biodiversity. Meadows are also good for insect pollinators, especially if they contain a mix of native species. Every little square counts, so an easy hack is to create a meadow in a pot. It requires almost no maintenance and is both stylish as well as a fun and unexpected gift! What's more, it will attract insects to your vegetable garden, allowing you to maximise your harvest.

YOU WILL NEED

→ a few handfuls of rocks
→ a bunch of sticks
→ a large pot with a hole in the bottom
→ nutrient-poor soil (which wildflowers thrive in)
→ water
→ wildflower seeds
→ sand or gravel (optional)

STEP BY STEP

1. Put some rocks and sticks in the bottom of the pot. This makes for better drainage.

2. Fill the pot with nutrient-poor soil, mixing it with the sticks and rocks before watering.

3. Sow your seeds, either ones that you have collected from another meadow or that you have bought (but choose native species).

4. Add some sand, gravel or more nutrient-poor soil and wait.

Spring

Tomato Twist

→ Tomatoes need support, and this clever design also allows for deep watering. The plastic pipe I have used is similar to the kind often mounted under a sink.

→ handsaw
→ a plastic pipe, preferably more than 1 metre (3¼ feet) long and 3 cm (1¼ inches) in diameter
→ drill and spade bit with the same diameter as the hose, about 20 mm (¾ inch) is standard
→ a piece of garden hose, about 1.5 metres (5 feet) long
→ a large pot with a hole in the bottom
→ soil

STEP BY STEP

1. Cut the plastic pipe to the appropriate length if necessary, depending on the expected height of the plant.
2. Drill holes straight through the pipe. Repeat along the entire pipe at intervals of about 20 cm (8 inches).
3. Thread the hose through the holes to create a spiral shape.
4. Stand the pipe and hose in a pot.
5. Add soil to stabilise the structure.
6. Plant a tomato in the centre of the spiral. As it grows, it will be able to lean on the hose.
7. When watering, pour the water into the plastic pipe. This way, the water reaches all the way to the bottom of the pot.

Robust Rebar Plant Support

→ Some plants need a little more support, and for a small amount of money you can easily make your own. They are very strong, age beautifully like corten steel and blend in well with your garden. What's more, they are very quick to make.

YOU WILL NEED

→ pencil
→ a piece of rebar, 2 metres (6½ feet) long and 8 mm (⅜ inch) thick
→ tape measure
→ gloves
→ vice or something hard for bending the rebar

STEP BY STEP

1. Draw two marks on the rebar, about 65 cm (25½ inches) from one end and then 65 cm (25½ inches) from the other.
2. Using a vice or something hard, bend the rebar 90 degrees at both points, making sure that the ends are parallel. You have now made a completely straight support shaped like a football goal.
3. You can stick the ends in the ground and use the support as it is, but I usually like to make it rounded, so that the support embraces the plant.
4. Bend the top a little against something hard at 10 cm (4 inch) intervals until you have achieved the desired shape.
5. Stick the ends firmly into the soil next to the plant. Lift the plant and adjust it to ensure proper support.

Spring

Moveable Climbing Frame

→ One nice thing about legumes is that they have special bacteria in their roots that collect nitrogen gas from the air and convert it into forms of nitrogen that plants can absorb. This is known as nitrogen fixation. You'll want to move your legumes around each year so that other plants can benefit from the nitrogen in the soil. At the same time, you'll need something for your legumes to climb on, and it can be a hassle to rebuild it in a new location. The solution is a moveable climbing frame!

YOU WILL NEED

→ two pieces of welded wire mesh, 2.35 × 1.25 metres (7¾ × 4 feet) with 20 cm (8 inch) squares
→ steel wire, 1 metre (3¼ feet) long
→ wire cutters
→ two wooden planks, 1 metre (3¼ feet) long and at least 5 cm (2 inches) wide
→ pencil
→ drill and drill bit
→ a saw (optional)

STEP BY STEP

1. Place the two pieces of wire mesh so they lean against each other to form an upside-down V, with the long sides against the ground and along the top.
2. Tie them together at the top using steel wire. Do this at every other square, so that the top edge holds together when they are leaning against each other but the whole thing can easily be folded up if you lift the mesh.
3. Place the mesh at the appropriate angle for the chosen garden bed.
4. Hold one wooden plank against the short side of the mesh, parallel to the ground, in line with the third square from the top. With the plank in place, the whole thing should look like an A.
5. Mark where the ends of the third square meet the plank. At the mark,

→

drill a hole so that the ends of the mesh can slot into the plank, thus locking the structure into shape.

6. Repeat steps 4 and 5 at the opposite end of the structure. Slot the mesh ends into the planks and lock the structure into shape. If necessary, saw off the ends of the planks so they don't stick out too much.

7. When you need to move the climbing frame, simply unhook the planks on one side and fold the frame up along with the planks. Easy-peasy!

Rickety Fence

→ Some thin and gangly plants can be tricky to grow in a pot. With a piece of fencing or chicken wire, you can prepare and avoid having to use sticks to tie up the plant later.

YOU WILL NEED

→ a piece of garden fence, 1.2 metres (4 feet) high with 10 × 5 cm (4 × 2 inch) mesh
→ a pot with a hole in the bottom
→ wire cutters
→ soil

STEP BY STEP

1. Wrap the garden fence around the pot and cut it so there are wires sticking out along one short side. These will be used to tie the fence together. The length of the fence should be slightly bigger than the inner circumference of the pot.

2. Push the fence down into the pot and bend each protruding wire around the wire on the other short side of the fence to make a tube that holds together.

3. Pour soil into the pot to stabilise the fence and plant in. Sow seeds or plant seedlings and let them climb up the rickety fence.

Climbing Tree

→ There is something about big potted plants. If you want to quickly create a big potted plant with plenty of volume, you can do so by using a branch that you secure in a pot. With a fast-growing climbing plant, you'll have a miniature tree in no time!

YOU WILL NEED

→ handsaw
→ a wooden board, at least 10 × 10 cm (4 × 4 inches)
→ a large pot
→ drill and 10 mm (½ inch) drill bit
→ screwdriver and screws
→ a branch or piece of driftwood
→ rocks
→ soil
→ climbing plant

STEP BY STEP

1. Saw a round or square wooden board to make a plate that fits inside the bottom of the pot.
2. Drill several holes in the plate for some drainage.
3. Screw the plate to the base of the branch with a few screws.
4. Place the plate with the branch in the pot and stabilise it by putting some rocks on the plate.
5. Add soil and plant your climbing plant.
6. Carefully guide the climbing plant onto the branch.

Summer

Now all the plants in your garden are racing to take advantage of the warmth and the light, and there are various ways that you can help maximise their yield. These can be indirect, such as helping pollinators, but also more tangible measures, such as fertilising and harvesting – yes, the latter actually leads to a bigger harvest!

And it's not just humans who like to enjoy the fruits, vegetables and flowers of summer. Animals and insects love our gardens at this time of year too, and they should have their fill. But sometimes too many of them gather in the wrong place. Then, it's important to protect your plants in a good way. Buying everything you need can be expensive but by making a lot of things yourself and using objects and materials originally intended for other purposes, you can often take good, cheap shortcuts!

Combined Bee Hotel and Street Number Sign

→ You can never have too many bee hotels, and if you can combine it with a nice street number sign, there is really nothing to think about! The latest research I have read says that it's best to drill the holes perpendicular to the wood fibres, take care not to leave any splinters at the openings, use several types of drill bits – from the thinnest to the thickest – and to vary the depth of the holes. If you do this, you'll have a high occupancy rate and maximise the number of different insect species in your hotel!

YOU WILL NEED

→ a thicker piece of wood, such as a log split in half, preferably more than 10 cm (4 inches) thick
→ chalk
→ drill and different-sized drill bits

STEP BY STEP

1. Write your street number on the piece of wood with chalk. This will serve as a guide for where to drill the holes.
2. Drill lots of holes along the chalk lines, varying their size and depth.
3. Hang the combined hotel and street number sign in a way that suits the material in your house wall. Researchers recommend hanging it on a south or southeast-facing wall, but I have guests staying in hotels on north-facing walls, too!

Summer

Pollinate with a Make-up Brush

→ In a greenhouse or on a balcony, there may be little wind and few bees. If so, you can pollinate the plants yourself to maximise your harvest. The easiest way to do this is with a make-up brush attached to an electric toothbrush. That way, you mimic a bee by vibrating while brushing the centre of the flower (i.e. the pistil). The pollen that sticks to the brush is then passed on to the next flower. This increases the likelihood of a good harvest!

YOU WILL NEED
→ electric toothbrush
→ make-up brush
→ tape

STEP BY STEP
1. Remove the toothbrush head from the electric toothbrush and place the handle of the make-up brush against the spike of the electric toothbrush instead.
2. Tape the brush to the metal spike. Add a few extra layers of tape to ensure that the make-up brush is firmly attached.
3. Turn on the toothbrush and gently insert the make-up brush into a flower.
4. Brush lightly.
5. Move on to the next flower and repeat.

Clog-free Fertiliser Tea

→ As summer kicks in, we need to replenish the soil with nutrients. Both chicken manure and nettle tea are fast-acting and natural, but also quite strong. A good trick is therefore to dilute them with water. Use a laundry pouch to avoid clumps clogging up the nozzle.

YOU WILL NEED
→ watering can
→ water
→ a laundry, produce or other type of mesh bag
→ chicken manure or nettles

STEP BY STEP
1. Fill the can with water.
2. Fill the bag with chicken manure or nettles and drop it into the watering can.
3. Leave to soak for 24 hours before watering your plants.
4. After watering, you can refill the can with more water and let it soak again. After a week or so, add new nettles or chicken manure to the bag.

Summer

Bag-in-box Nutrient Container

→ Nutrient solutions can have a slight odour and are often difficult to pour in the right dose. The bag-in-box nutrient container makes everything much easier! All you need is a bag-in-box (BiB) bag from a box of wine or other liquid, a sealing clip and a hook and your struggle is a thing of the past.

YOU WILL NEED

→ scissors
→ an empty BiB bag
→ awl
→ S-hook
→ nutrient solution
→ sealing clip

STEP BY STEP

1. Cut off the corner of the BiB bag, directly above the tap. In other words, if the tap is on the bottom right, cut off the top-right corner. This will be your refill hole.
2. In the opposite top corner, make a hole with the awl between the glue strips. Push the S-hook through the hole. Holding the S-hook, the bag should hang with the tap at the bottom. This allows as much liquid as possible to flow out if you open it.
3. Top up your nutrient solution through the refill hole.
4. Close the hole with the sealing clip.
5. Hang the bag in a suitable spot using the S-hook.

Three Ways to Avoid Ants

→ Ants like hot weather, so they come in droves in the summer. And it's not always fun to have them in your pots. They dig away soil and make it dry out faster. Cloth, cinnamon and water sounds like a recipe – but that's all you need! A barrier, a strong odour and moisture. The different methods can be used separately but are most effective when combined. Before you start, however, it's a good idea to check your plant for aphids. Ants can be a sign of an infestation, as they love the sweet secretion that aphids leave behind. They have even been known to protect the aphids to secure their source of food!

YOU WILL NEED

→ a mosquito net, 5 × 5 cm (2 × 2 inches)
→ a pot with a hole in the bottom
→ a pot saucer (optional)
→ ground cinnamon
→ soil
→ water

STEP BY STEP

1. Place the mosquito net over the drainage hole in the bottom of the pot.
2. Sprinkle some cinnamon on the bottom and on the saucer (if you have one). Ants do not like strong smells.
3. Add soil and your plant.
4. Water frequently to keep the soil moist. Ants like it dry. If you have a saucer, you can water that way; it creates a small moat that the ants will struggle to get past.

Summer

Sturdy Strawberry Cage

→ Birds like berries, but classic bird netting often turns into a tangled, miserable mess. An option is to use an upside-down wire basket instead, but sometimes it can be difficult to find one the right size for your garden bed. If so, you can build a cage out of chicken wire! It can easily be lifted and moved around by you – but not by the birds. It's also a bit more stylish.

YOU WILL NEED

→ handsaw (optional)
→ wooden slats, two 100 cm (39½ inches) long and two 70 cm (27½ inches) long
→ drill and 3 mm (⅛ inch) drill bit
→ screwdriver and 6 cm (2½ inch) long screws
→ staple gun
→ chicken wire (30 cm/12 inch wider and longer than the frame, so for this you need 130 × 100 cm/ 51 × 39½ inches)
→ wire cutters

STEP BY STEP

1. Saw the slats for the frame if necessary, so you have two long sides and two short sides with dimensions to fit your garden bed.
2. Drill pilot holes for the screws in the corners of each short side. Screw the frame together (see page 69).
3. Staple one short side of the chicken wire to one short side of the frame. Make sure there is 15 cm (6 inches) of chicken wire sticking out on each side.
4. Repeat on the other side.
5. Make a 15 cm (6 inch) cut from the long side in one corner, so that the wire sticking out from the short side becomes a foldable square to create a neat corner. Repeat in all four corners.
6. Bend and staple the two long sides of the chicken wire to the slat frame.
7. Finally, bend the wire so that the corner overlaps on the long side and staple it to the frame.

Summer

Summer

A Cage for Your Currants

→ As your berries begin to ripen, the birds' mouths begin to water. I've grown tired of traditional bird netting – birds and hedgehogs get stuck and it's just impractical. Instead, I secure my black- and redcurrant jelly by putting a tube of chicken wire around my bush and a wire basket on top! What's more, unlike bird netting, chicken wire can be reused year after year. The wire can easily be removed when it's time to harvest, and next year you can increase the diameter of the tube if the bush has grown.

YOU WILL NEED

→ chicken wire (the width of the wire becomes the height of the tube and the length is determined by the circumference of the bush)
→ steel wire
→ wire cutters
→ wire basket (optional)

STEP BY STEP

1. Wrap the chicken wire right around the bush.
2. Using steel wire, tie the edges together so that the chicken wire forms a tube.
3. Add a wire basket as a roof (if you have one), or put a piece of chicken wire over the top of the tube and secure it with steel wire. When it's time to harvest, just lift the top.

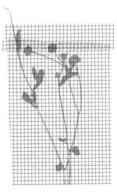

Potted Plant Protection

→ Sometimes you may need to protect your potted plants from rabbits, deer or birds. If so, an upside-down mesh wastepaper bin can help! It protects the plant, while also letting through water and sunlight.

YOU WILL NEED

→ a mesh wastepaper bin
→ a rock

STEP BY STEP

1. Turn the bin upside down.
2. Place it over your potted plant, on the edge of the pot or just inside.
3. Put a rock on top to keep it in place.

Summer

Scare Away Birds with a Snake in Your Garden

→ Birds can be quite annoying when you are trying to grow things in your garden. They pick at berries, scatter seeds and tear away covers in search of worms. There is no single deterrent that always works, but alternating between different ones and moving them around can keep birds away from certain sensitive areas. A regular rubber snake from my nearest toy shop that I move around each day works well for me!

YOU WILL NEED

→ a rubber snake

STEP BY STEP

1. Place the snake in a spot where it's clearly visible, preferably on a bright surface.
2. Move the snake frequently (otherwise the birds get used to it).

Protect Your Potting Soil

→ Potting soil benefits from protection, too. With pine cones or shards from broken pots, you can cover the soil to slow evaporation, prevent weeds and create a stylish surface to boot. Terracotta shards give a Mediterranean feel with no need to hop on a plane!

YOU WILL NEED

→ pine cones or shards from a broken pot

STEP BY STEP

1. Cover the soil around the plant with pine cones or shards. If it's a tree, you'll want to leave some space between the trunk and the covering material. Otherwise, there is a risk that the soil will be too moist and that fungus may begin to grow.

Summer

Reach Your Bushes with a Watering and Nutrient Tube

→ Struggling with back pain? Don't want your tomatoes to be infected with late blight? Want the nutrients for your bushes to end up where they are actually needed? Then a watering and nutrient tube is just what you need! Stick it into bushes or dense plants for easier access and add water and nutrients without having to bend over and struggle, only to get everything on the leaves and in the wrong place.

YOU WILL NEED

- → handsaw
- → a plastic pipe (a ventilation, sewage or drainpipe works well)
- → drill and 10 mm (½ inch) drill bit
- → rope, at least 1 cm (½ inch) thick and about 40 cm (16 inches) longer than the pipe
- → nutrient solution or water

STEP BY STEP

1. Cut the pipe to the right length; it should reach from your elbow to the ground. I find about 1.2 metres (4 feet) to be good, but it depends on how tall you are.
2. Cut the ends of the pipe to create an angled opening on each side (see image opposite).
3. Drill holes for the rope a few centimetres from each end.
4. Thread the rope through the holes and tie a knot on the inside.
5. Now you can hold the rope and stick the pipe into bushes or down near the ground. Pour the nutrient solution or water through the pipe and guide it to the right place.

A Tap for Your Watering Can

→ Us gardening folk like to get our hands dirty. And if you have an allotment, the nearest water source may not be that close. This nifty mobile water tap makes hand washing much easier!

- → drill and spade drill bit (20 mm/¾ inch is standard for water butt taps)
- → a water butt tap (often sold for rain barrels)
- → plastic watering can
- → water

STEP BY STEP

1. Drill a hole that exactly matches the diameter of the water butt tap just below the handle on the back of your watering can.
2. Push the tap through the hole with the gasket on the outside and screw it in place on the inside of the watering can.
3. Fill up the watering can with water. Open the tap and wash your hands!

Summer

Keep Your Hose Organised

→ Does your hose reel always turn into a mess? Ever get your hose stuck under a raised garden bed after decapitating the peonies? Trust me, you are not alone. Secure the hose reel with a bent rebar and place small wooden posts along flower beds and corners where the hose can run. That way, watering becomes a joy again!

YOU WILL NEED

→ two pieces of rebar, one for each leg of the hose reel
→ hammer or mallet
→ garden hose reel
→ digging bar
→ branches or posts, at least 40 cm (16 inches) long and 5 cm (2 inches) thick, how many depends on the number of awkward spots in your garden you want to secure

STEP BY STEP

1. Bend each rebar over something hard to form a U-shape (the looser the soil, the longer the legs need to be).

2. With the hammer or mallet, strike the bent pieces of rebar into the ground over the leg of the hose reel (at both the back and front for better stability).

3. Make holes with the digging bar in suitable places around your garden where the hose tends to get stuck or accidentally caught on flowers and other plants. This could be around flower beds or in front of the hose reel.

4. Strike the posts into the holes and let the hose run around them instead of sliding over into the flower bed or getting stuck on corners.

Summer

Simple Irrigation Stand

→ Often, you'll want to focus your watering for a long time in one spot to really saturate the soil and plants. But we all know how boring that is. So on the hot days of summer, you need to be clever. With some steel wire, a pot and a stick, you can make an irrigation stand and go do something else instead.

YOU WILL NEED
→ steel wire, about 30 cm (12 inches) long
→ a stick, about 6 cm (2½ inches) long
→ a pot with a hole in the bottom
→ garden hose

STEP BY STEP
1. Fold the steel wire over the stick and wrap to secure.
2. Place the stick in the pot and tuck the two ends of the wire through the drainage hole (see image on page 86).
3. Turn the pot upside down and place it on the ground.
4. Wrap the steel wire around the nozzle of the hose. The stick holds the steel wire in place, stabilising the contraption. Just point the nozzle and turn on the water!

Summer

Summer

Face Mask Hammock

→ Left-over face masks from the pandemic or regular dust masks can serve a whole new function. Use them to support big hanging fruits, such as melons or calabashes!

YOU WILL NEED

→ fine string or garden twine
→ a face or dust mask

STEP BY STEP

1. Secure the string to fixed points that can carry the weight of the fruit, such as rafters in the greenhouse ceiling.
2. Tie the string to the face or dust mask.
3. Place the mask under the fruit to provide support.

Smart Herb Garden

→ When buying potted herbs from the supermarket, we rarely use the whole plant. Often, we harvest only half, while the rest wilts by our kitchen window. Instead, prepare a pot (or a bucket with a hole in it) and replant the herbs immediately after using what you need. After a few dinners, you'll soon have an entire herb garden and no need to go to the shop!

YOU WILL NEED

→ a large pot with a hole in the bottom
→ garden soil
→ herbs from the supermarket

STEP BY STEP

1. Fill up the pot with garden soil.
2. Plant the root ball with what's left of the herb in the pot.
3. Add more types of herbs when you have root balls left over from your cooking.

Summer

Rapid Herb Harvesting

→ This clever trick makes picking fresh herbs so much quicker and easier. All you need is a colander!

YOU WILL NEED
→ colander

STEP BY STEP

1. Stick the end of the herb stem into one of the holes in the colander from the inside.
2. Pull the stem through the hole.
3. The leaves will fall into the colander and the stem can be thrown directly onto the compost pile.

Maximise the Flavour of Dried Herbs

→ In early summer, herbs are at their best. This is the time to harvest if you want to maximise the flavour and avoid that bitter taste that develops later in the season when they flower. If you dry your herbs right, you can enjoy the taste of summer well into the winter! The easiest way is just to hang them up, but then they risk getting dusty and dried leaves may fall to the floor. A useful trick instead is to hang them in mesh bags for storing produce. However, the best method is to dry them in a paper bag, which also keeps out the light. This preserves the flavours better.

YOU WILL NEED

→ scissors
→ any small paper bag
→ herbs
→ a piece of string
→ jar with an airtight lid

STEP BY STEP

1. Cut small holes in the paper bag. This is to create some ventilation – you don't want any mould.
2. Harvest the herbs and tie them into a small bouquet.
3. Insert the bouquet into the bag, leaving part of the stems sticking out.
4. Tie the bag around the stems and make a loop on the string to hang it up.
5. Hang the bag in a dry place, out of direct sunlight. Wait three to five days for the herbs to dry, then use them straight away or transfer them into a tightly sealed jar.

Summer

Fly-proof Your Tomatoes

→ You can let your tomatoes ripen indoors, but you might have a problem with fruit flies. Avoid this by hanging them in a fine mesh produce bag.

YOU WILL NEED

→ a mesh produce bag

STEP BY STEP

1. Place your unripe tomatoes in the mesh bag.
2. If you have harvested a vine or cluster, leave the branch sticking out and tie the bag around it. This allows the tomatoes to hang freely inside the bag, reducing the risk of bruising.
3. Hang the bag, avoiding direct sunlight to make sure that they retain their juiciness and soft skins.

Autumn

The days are growing colder, the evenings are getting darker and the plants are wilting. Many people see autumn as the end of the growing season, but I think of it as the beginning! This is when you really get to enjoy the fruits of all that hard work over the summer. It means you'll need to find smart ways to gather and prepare your harvest for storage. This is also the time to bring in many of your tools and utensils, to show them some love and make any repairs. And to collect seeds for next season. I also do some sowing. For instance, meadows and lawns are great to start up in autumn! And don't forget all the bulbs and other things that should be planted this time of year so that they can come up in early spring and provide food for the bees. Now that the intense and hectic growing season is over, there is also time to tinker with and build things to simplify your gardening next summer, and – perhaps most importantly – there is an opportunity to improve and care for the soil to prepare it for winter and another season full of life!

Paperback
Mushrooms

→ If you are hooked on the thrill of watching things grow, you can continue to grow food indoors through the autumn. With some mycelium and a paperback, you can grow mushrooms at home. Mushroom mycelium can be ordered online, and I'm sure you have an old detective novel you have already read lying around … It'll last you three harvests before it's time to change the book!

YOU WILL NEED

→ a paperback, at least 200 pages but preferably more
→ large bowl of lukewarm water
→ mushroom mycelium (comes either 'pure' or as 'spawn', i.e. grown on something like wheat grains, both are fine)
→ two sturdy rubber bands to go round the book without being too tight (leave room for the mycelium!)

STEP BY STEP

1. Soak the paperback in a bowl of lukewarm water for about 20 minutes, until completely wet.
2. Press out any excess water by squeezing the book tightly with your hands a few times.
3. Put a thin layer of mushroom mycelium at 50-page intervals throughout the book. Spread the mycelium over the entire page.
4. Close the book and put the rubber bands over it, so that the pages are held together firmly.
5. Place the book inside a plastic bag and seal it tightly.
6. Leave the book indoors in a place that is bright but out of direct sunlight for two weeks. The mushroom mycelium will begin to spread like a white, fuzzy web.

- → plastic bag, large enough to hold the book
- → spray bottle
- → water

7. After two weeks, move the bag with the book to the fridge for two days. This initiates the mushroom's growth in earnest.

8. Remove the book from the fridge and open the bag. Fold down the plastic bag so that only half the book is covered. Place the book with the spine down and the pages up in a bright spot indoors, but out of direct sunlight.

9. Spray the book with water every day to keep it moist. In a couple of weeks, it will be time to harvest! After harvesting, you can continue spraying; often you can get as many as three rounds of mushrooms from one book.

Autumn

Grass Seed Spreader

→ Autumn is a good time to fill in bald patches or holes in your lawn, as the evenings and nights are more humid, there is more rain and fewer competing weeds. To avoid the grass seeds sticking together in clumps, use this simple super-seeding aid: the plastic tomato container!

YOU WILL NEED
→ grass seed
→ an empty plastic tomato container with 4–6 holes in the bottom

STEP BY STEP
1. Pour the grass seed into the plastic tomato container.
2. Shake the container over the parts of your lawn that you wish to improve. This disperses the seeds at an appropriate distance, leaving the lawn nice and even.

Simple Pot Rack

→ Looking for a way to stack your pots neatly and easily, which is moveable and prevents them from sticking together? A rough plank and some rebar will do the trick!

→ pots
→ a rough plank, at least 5 cm (2 inches) thick, preferably more
→ pencil
→ three pieces of rebar, 40 cm (16 inches) long and 8–10 mm (⅜–½ inch) in diameter
→ drill and drill bit, the dimensions will depend on the thickness of the rebar
→ hammer
→ some cardboard you have lying around

STEP BY STEP

1. Place three pots upside down on the plank. Make sure they fit without touching each other. With a pencil, draw around the edges of the pots on the plank to mark their placement. I chose to put two pots next to each other and one pot behind, in a triangle formation.

2. Draw a cross in the centre of each circle. This is where you will place the rebar.

3. At each cross, drill a hole halfway down into the plank. Make sure not to drill all the way through and that the holes have a slightly smaller diameter than the rebar, otherwise they won't sit firmly.

4. Strike each piece of rebar down with a hammer so that they point straight up out of the plank.

5. Then stack the pots upside down, with the rebar sticking up through the drainage holes. Place a piece of cardboard between each pot to prevent them from sticking together.

Autumn

Simple Onion-drying Trick

→ When the haulm (stem) begins to bend, it's a clear sign that it is time to harvest your onions. Use your garden furniture to quickly and easily dry the onions for storage.

YOU WILL NEED

→ garden furniture with a slatted seat

STEP BY STEP

1. Harvest your onions but leave the haulm on, otherwise there is a high risk that the onions will rot.
2. Place the onions with the roots up and haulm down between the slats of your garden furniture.
3. Place the furniture in the sun, preferably in a spot with a breeze and good air circulation.
4. Leave to dry in the sun for about two weeks. Bring the onions inside if it starts to rain.
5. After two weeks, you can peel off the dirty, outer layer of skin with your hands and store the onions in a cool, dry place indoors, or braid and hang them in your kitchen.

Tarpaulin for Trimmings

→ When it comes to clearing away brushwood in the garden, the tarpaulin is my best friend. Especially if I need to remove thorny branches, such as blackberry trimmings. Pile on all the trimmings, cut them into smaller pieces and drag them where they need to go. There is no end to how much a tarpaulin can swallow, and this way you don't have to pick up all the rubbish!

YOU WILL NEED

→ a rope, 2 metres (6½ feet) long
→ a tarpaulin (with eyelets), about 2 metres (6½ feet) square

STEP BY STEP

1. Tie the rope to the two eyelets on one short side of the tarpaulin.
2. Pile on the trimmings and brushwood.
3. Wait to cut the material into smaller pieces until it's on the tarpaulin to avoid spreading it everywhere.
4. Drag everything to your compost pile or rubbish bin.

Autumn

Save Water When Rinsing Your Harvest

→ I like to rinse my vegetables before bringing them into the kitchen. An old bicycle basket holds a lot and if you rinse your harvest over a bucket, the water can be recovered and used for irrigation.

YOU WILL NEED

→ bicycle basket
→ large bucket

STEP BY STEP

1. As you harvest, place your vegetables in the bicycle basket.
2. Place the basket over a bucket.
3. Rinse the vegetables, collecting the run-off in the bucket.

Goodbye to Sharp Bucket Handles

→ You can never have too many buckets! I use them for weeds, soil, sand and tools. But some buckets don't have the best handle – sometimes it's hardly more than a steel wire. With the help of an old hose and some pliers, you can easily make it comfortable to carry!

YOU WILL NEED

→ pliers
→ a piece of garden hose, three-quarters the length of the bucket handle

STEP BY STEP

1. Where the handle is attached to the bucket, there is usually a small bend or hook that fits into a hole or loop on the bucket.
2. Pry open the hook at one end so that the handle can be unhooked from the bucket. (The other end can remain attached.)
3. Using the pliers, straighten the end of the metal handle.
4. Cut a piece of garden hose about three-quarters the length of the handle and thread it onto the metal.
5. Bend the metal handle end back into its original shape.
6. Reattach the handle to the bucket and make sure it's firmly attached.

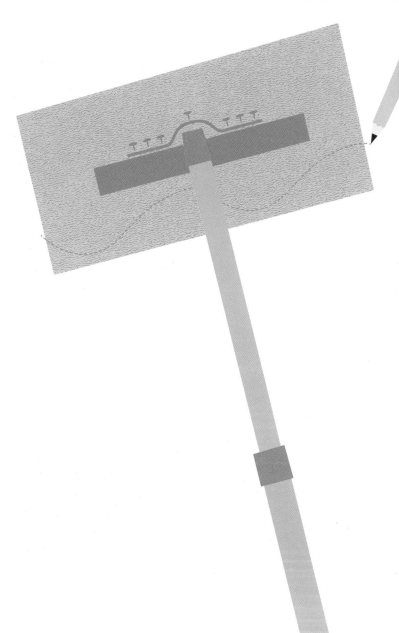

Autumn

Custom-made Moss Scraper

→ It's common to have moss growing on the roof. To prevent roof tiles from staying damp for a long time and perhaps cracking in freezing temperatures, it's good to get rid of it. At the same time, you'll want to avoid chemicals, especially if you collect run-off from the roof to water your plants. It is therefore best to do it manually. To make it a little more fun and easy, you can make a simple scraper that is tailored to your roof!

YOU WILL NEED

→ a wooden board, such as plywood, 20 × 40 cm (8 × 16 inches) and at least 2 cm (¾ inch) thick
→ pencil
→ jigsaw
→ hammer and 4 cm (1½ inch) long thin nails
→ a slat, about 20 cm (8 inches) long
→ a telescopic handle
→ a piece of fixing band, about 10 cm (4 inches) long

STEP BY STEP

1. The first thing is to draw the profile of your roof. Climb up to the eaves and hold the board against the tiles or metal. Trace the profile onto the board.

2. Saw it out with a jigsaw. I have made a profile for tiles on one side and corrugated iron on the other, so I can simply flip it around and use the same scraper on all my roofs.

3. Nail the slat to the middle of the board.

4. Place the telescopic handle so that it rests on the slat with one end right up against the board. Nail down the fixing band so that it wraps around the handle, then nail it to the slat on both sides of the handle, putting a nail through the band and the handle as well to really make it secure.

5. Staying safely on the ground, extend the handle and scrape away the moss.

Gutter-cleaning Wand

→ Cleaning the gutters may not be one of the great pleasures of autumn, but having your own tool made from a toy shovel and a toilet brush makes it a bit more fun!

- → drill and 5 mm (¼ inch) drill bit
- → a wooden shaft, such as a broom handle, 1.5 metres (5 feet) long
- → a toilet brush
- → a toy shovel
- → two bolts, 5 cm (2 inches) long and 5 mm (¼ inch) in diameter, with nuts

STEP BY STEP

1. Drill holes at both ends of the wooden shaft and at the end of the handle on the toilet brush and the shovel.
2. Push one of the bolts through the shovel and then through the wooden shaft. Tighten it with a nut that fits the bolt. At the other end of the wooden shaft, do the same with the toilet brush.
3. Turn the shovel so that it's at a good angle to be able to clean the gutter when you are standing on the ground.
4. Move the shovel through the gutter all the way to the end.
5. Flip the shaft around and repeat with the toilet brush to remove the last of the debris. Once you have pushed all of it to the end of the gutter, it's easy to remove and add to your compost pile.

Autumn

Clean and Oil Your Tools with Ease

→ If you are like me and don't always keep your garden tools in a garage or shed, they can get rusty and wear out pretty quickly. But there is a simple trick to take care of cleaning and oiling. Stick the tools in a bucket of sand and rapeseed oil after use! The sand cleans and sharpens the tools and the oil lubricates and protects.

YOU WILL NEED

→ sand (enough to fill the bucket to 80 per cent)
→ bucket
→ about 100 ml (3½ fl oz) rapeseed or vegetable oil (if it's a large bucket, use a little more)
→ spade

STEP BY STEP

1. Pour the sand into the bucket.
2. Add the oil and mix everything together with a spade.
3. Shove down your spades, hand rakes, trowels and the like.
4. It will last for at least a few seasons, until the bucket contains too much soil. Then, you can use the old sand for cuttings and make a new batch!

Clean Your Garden Hose

→ Over time, build up of iron, lime and dirt can easily form inside your garden hose, but these can be removed. Cut a small piece of sponge and flush it through the hose! But don't let it travel through hose reels, nozzles and connectors that are too narrow or have spirals where the sponge can get stuck.

YOU WILL NEED

→ scissors
→ sponge

STEP BY STEP

1. Cut off a small corner of the sponge, about 5 mm (¼ inch) square (not too big, or it may get stuck).
2. Disconnect all hose reels, nozzles and connectors from the hose.
3. Push the small corner of the sponge into one end of the hose, making sure there are no kinks or bends.
4. Attach a connector to the end where you inserted the sponge and connect the hose to the tap.
5. Turn the water on high and let the sponge pass through the hose and out the other end.
6. Repeat a few times for proper cleaning.

Spice Jar Seed Storage

→ I like to collect seeds in both summer and autumn and want to store them in a smart way. An old spice jar is perfect. It's a handy size and easy to open, reseal and get the right amount of seeds out. If you add a small desiccant sachet from a shoe or electronics box and put the jar in a dark place, you'll have made the ideal seed storage!

YOU WILL NEED
→ seeds
→ a clean, empty spice jar
→ a desiccant sachet

STEP BY STEP
1. Clean the seeds of leaves and dirt before pouring them into the spice jar.
2. Drop in a small desiccant sachet.
3. Store in a dark and preferably cool place until you're ready to use.

Coffee Filter Soil Barrier

→ In the autumn, many plants need to be brought back inside after spending the summer outside, and there will be some repotting to do. Why not seize the opportunity to make a few improvements! With a potted plant, you want the soil to stay in the pot, not spill out onto the windowsill. If you have forgotten to water your plant and the soil is so dry that the water runs straight through it, a soil barrier is a good idea. Place a coffee filter in the bottom of the pot. It holds the water back a little and prevents the soil particles from being washed out.

YOU WILL NEED
→ a coffee filter
→ a pot with a hole in the bottom
→ soil

STEP BY STEP
1. Place the coffee filter in the bottom of the pot so that it covers the drainage hole.
2. Add soil – and your pot is ready for planting.

Autumn

Revitalise Old Potting Soil

→ Soil should never be thrown away. It should be returned to the plants, but may need a little boost and reboot. Potting soil that is full of roots and poor in nutrients can actually be revitalised quite easily. Pour it into a raised garden bed or box in the autumn and add some ingredients that you probably already have in your garden. Come spring, it will be full of life once more!

YOU WILL NEED

→ a raised garden bed
→ old potting soil
→ used barbecue charcoal (not briquettes or ashes)
→ nutrients in the form of leachate, urine or nettle tea
→ worms (can be excluded if none are found)
→ mulch

STEP BY STEP

1. Place the garden bed directly on the ground. In other words, don't put any fabric or similar in the bottom.
2. Pour your old potting soil into the garden bed. Don't worry about removing roots; they will become food for the worms.
3. Add a few pieces of charcoal and some nutrient solution. The proportions of the different 'ingredients' aren't very important – just wing it!
4. Dig around in your garden for some worms and drop them into the garden bed.
5. Finally, add a layer of mulch for protection.

Worm Casting Tea

→ Worm castings are high in micro life and good nutrients, and are sold by the bag – at quite a hefty price. But you can pick them for free on your own lawn, if only you know what to look for! Worm castings look like small brown mounds, almost resembling mud, and are mostly found after it has rained and especially during autumn and winter when the heavy rains come. Add the worm castings directly to pots and garden beds or brew worm casting tea and distribute it that way.

YOU WILL NEED
→ bucket
→ watering can
→ water
→ a mesh jewellery bag (optional)

STEP BY STEP

1. Pick up the small piles of worm castings from your lawn and place them in the bucket.
2. Fill your watering can with water and add some of the worm castings in a mesh bag if you like. That way, the nutrients will dissolve without the risk of the castings getting clogged in the nozzle. Let the worm castings soak overnight before watering your plants.

Winter

By the time winter arrives, most of your garden will have been harvested, the plants that need protection from the cold have hopefully already been taken care of, and a stillness descends over the garden that is never really felt during other seasons. It's a stark contrast to springtime, when there is plenty to do – almost too much … Then, it's easy to feel stressed and overwhelmed. But that feeling can be alleviated by using winter to think of clever solutions, tools, contraptions and other fun things to simplify the work that lies ahead. Spend some time in your little workshop, thinking about what you need and what you can do better.

If your green fingers are getting too itchy, don't forget the plants that you actually can work on during winter – your indoor plants. You should also start propagating fairly soon if you want to get the most out of your garden (starting around Christmas if you're in the northern hemisphere). And let's not forget the birds; they should also be comfortable when the cold wind is blowing!

Wax Your Snow Shovel

→ At warmer temperatures where it still snows, like where I live in southern Sweden, snow is often a bit sticky. This can turn shovelling into heavy work, as the snow easily sticks to the shovel. The first thing you can do is leave the shovel outside so that it's cold when you start shovelling. If you leave it in a warm garage or shed, it can warm up the snow and make it even more difficult to shovel. If you want to take it a step further, add a little beeswax and the snow will slide right off. The wax can be used on both plastic and metal, and in the latter case it also acts as a little rustproofing!

YOU WILL NEED
→ water
→ washing-up liquid
→ wax (preferably beeswax)
→ cloth

STEP BY STEP
1. Wash the shovel with some water and washing-up liquid, then dry it.
2. Rub wax all over the blade and wipe off the excess with a cloth.
3. Leave the shovel outside and repeat if the snow starts to stick again.

Rope-and-stick Carrying System

→ When picking up debris after a storm or collecting firewood, you need something to carry it in. I find baskets to be impractical. Instead, I usually use a simple carrying system made from two sticks and two ropes. It's incredibly convenient!

YOU WILL NEED

→ drill and 10 mm (½ inch) drill bit
→ two sticks, 30 cm (12 inches) long
→ two equal lengths of rope or thick string, approx. 1.5 metres (5 feet) long and 1 cm (½ inch) thick

STEP BY STEP

1. Drill a hole 2 cm (¾ inch) from both ends of each stick.

2. Thread each rope through one hole on each stick. Make sure the ropes run parallel and do not cross if you lay them out. Tie a knot at each of the four ends.

3. Place the contraption on the ground and lay the ropes out straight. Place your wood or branches in the middle of the ropes.

4. Thread one of the handles (i.e. sticks) through the ropes on the other side, thus locking the wood/branches into place. Now you can lift the other handle, hoist it onto your shoulder and carry the load with ease (see image on page 140).

Winter

Plastic Bottle Bird Feeder

→ Small birds need a lot of food in winter, but also in spring and early summer when they raise their young. You can feed them throughout most of the year with sunflower seeds. Make a simple bird feeder using only a plastic bottle and a spoon. Hang it near trees and bushes so they don't have to leave their shelter or nest for too long to get food.

YOU WILL NEED

→ snap-off craft knife
→ a plastic bottle, 1.25 litres (¼ gallon)
→ a metal spoon (a regular tablespoon is a good size)
→ glue
→ birdseed
→ a piece of string

STEP BY STEP

1. Cut a hole 3 cm (1¼ inches) from the bottom of the bottle so that the bowl of the spoon just about fits. Make a small cut 7 cm (2¾ inches) from the bottom on the opposite side of the bottle so that the handle can be pushed through.

2. Insert the spoon with the handle first into the larger hole, leaving the ends of the bowl and handle sticking out on either side of the bottle (see image opposite). Put a small dab of glue where the spoon rests against the bottle at both ends to ensure that it's stable. It should be angled so the food can slide down the spoon and the birds can sit there and eat.

3. Fill the bottle with seeds (you could use the scoop on page 145). Close the cap.

4. Tie a piece of string around the bottle under the 'neck ring' near the top and hang close to bushes and trees.

Winter

Combined Scoop and Funnel

→ A scoop is a handy thing to have, especially when topping up your bird feeder. Make your own out of a plastic bottle and get a bonus feature! If you unscrew the cap, it turns into a scoop with a built-in funnel that makes it easy to fill bird feeders, even those with a narrow opening.

YOU WILL NEED

→ a clean, empty plastic bottle
→ pencil
→ snap-off craft knife

STEP BY STEP

1. Cut off the bottom of the bottle.
2. Draw a nice scoop shape by following the side of the bottle in a gentle curve up towards the handle. Do this on both sides of the bottle.
3. Cut along the line with the knife.
4. Smooth out any sharp edges.
5. Start scooping!

Give Your Christmas Tree a Second Life

→ When the holidays are over and you need the spot where the Christmas tree has been standing for early indoor propagation, it's time to give your tree a second life. Bring it out into your garden and let it serve as protection for perennials now and as a climbing tree for plants in the spring.

YOU WILL NEED
→ secateurs
→ a discarded Christmas tree
→ a large pot
→ rocks
→ soil
→ climbing plants, such as sweet pea

STEP BY STEP

1. Cut off all the branches on the tree.
2. Use the branches to cover the soil around your perennials. Loose needles can be spread out, too. They are particularly suitable for rhododendrons and blueberries that thrive in slightly acidic soil.
3. Put the trunk in a pot and place a few rocks in the bottom to make it stable. When spring comes, you can fill the pot with soil and sow or plant a climbing plant. Soon you'll have a summer tree to dance around!

Make Your Own Seed Tape

→ Small seeds can be difficult to sow with even spacing; they tend to end up in clumps. To prevent this, you can make your own seed tape! A bit of toilet paper, flour, water and seeds are all you need to prepare nice straight seed rows with even spacing long before the season begins.

YOU WILL NEED

→ seeds
→ a plate or similar
→ flour
→ water
→ small glass or jar
→ toilet paper
→ tape measure
→ pencil or wooden skewer

STEP BY STEP

1. Pour the seeds onto a small plate or directly onto the table.
2. Mix 2 tablespoons of flour with 1 tablespoon of water in a small glass (it shouldn't be too runny, more of a sticky batter).
3. Lay out toilet paper on the table or on the floor (the longer the better).
4. Fold the toilet paper lengthways and unfold again to make a crease in the middle that runs parallel to the long sides of the paper.
5. Lay out the tape measure along the toilet paper so that you can place the seeds at an even distance.
6. Dip the pencil or skewer into the flour mixture so that the tip becomes sticky, then dip it into the seeds so that one gets picked up.
7. Twist off the seed onto the toilet paper midway between one long side and the folded line.

8. Check the seed packet for the correct spacing. Do the same with the next seed, placing it at the specified distance from the first one.

9. When you have completed the entire length of toilet paper, apply some of the flour 'glue' at regular intervals along one edge of the paper.

10. Fold the paper along the original crease you made and roll it up. Allow to dry and don't forget to label your seed tape in some way.

11. Unroll the tape in a garden bed in spring, cover with soil and water it in well!

Smart Indoor Gardening Tools

→ Indoor gardening also requires tools, and smaller versions are often more convenient. You probably already have my favourites at home: cutlery, a stick, a plastic bottle and a screwdriver. The stick and the screwdriver, you don't even need to modify – they are useful as they are! With the stick, you can make holes for sowing and poke down seeds. Just moisten the tip, then pick up the seed and push it down into the soil. The screwdriver can be used to loosen up your potting soil. This is helpful when repotting and allows oxygen to reach the roots.

YOU WILL NEED
PLASTIC BOTTLE SCOOP:
- → **snap-off craft knife**
- → **a plastic bottle, 500 ml (17 fl oz)**
- → **pencil**

FORK RAKE:
- → **metal fork**
- → **pliers**

STEP BY STEP
PLASTIC BOTTLE SCOOP:
1. Cut off the bottom of the bottle.
2. Draw a nice scoop shape on the side of the bottle. Make sure that the edges aren't too low, so that the material you scoop up doesn't fall out.
3. Cut along the drawn lines with the knife.
4. Use the bottle neck and cap as a handle when, for example, scooping up soil as you replant your potted plants.

FORK RAKE:
1. Bend the teeth of the fork with the pliers so that the fork resembles a rake.
2. Use the rake to loosen up the topsoil of potted plants or to untangle the roots of seedlings that you are planning to divide and transplant.

→ **metal spoon**
→ **hacksaw**

MINI SPADE:

1. Actually, you can use the spoon as it is. But if you want to take it to the next level, saw out a mini spade using a hacksaw. Cut the shape according to taste. I cut my spoon so that the top half of the bowl is reduced to an extension of the handle. Suddenly you have a handy spade to use in your small seedling pots, to add some gravel or perlite to the top or to dig up small plants for repotting.

Winter

Microgreens in a Bottle Greenhouse

→ Microgreens have become very trendy. The word may sound high tech, but they're actually nothing more than delicate seedlings of regular plants. As they shoot up through the soil, they are bursting with nutrients. Not only are they delicious, they're good for you, too! And you can grow them for next to nothing. Skip the seeds from the garden centre; all you need can be found at the supermarket for a tenth of the price. A bag of pea shoots that costs £2–3 (US$2–4) in the shop can easily be grown at home for less than 10p (10c)! And with a mini greenhouse made from a bottle, there is hardly any labour involved. Just fill the base with water when you sow and the plant will take care of itself.

YOU WILL NEED

→ snap-off craft knife
→ a plastic bottle, 1.25 litres (¼ gallon)
→ awl or nail
→ discarded mop
→ scissors
→ a small pot, 10 cm (4 inches) in diameter, with a hole in the bottom
→ soil
→ water
→ seeds (see page 156)

STEP BY STEP

1. Cut off the top third of the plastic bottle. This will be the roof.
2. Make a hole in the bottle cap with the awl. This will act as a ventilation hole to prevent the mini greenhouse from getting too humid.
3. Cut one or two strands from the mop with the scissors. Tuck them halfway through the drainage hole in the pot.
4. Fill the pot with soil.
5. Half-fill the base of the bottle with water. Place the pot so that it hangs freely and the mop strands are submerged in the water.
6. Sow your seeds and put the top over the pot.

→

7. Leave on a windowsill for about 14 days (a grow light may be necessary during the darkest months of the year). The mop strands will absorb water to keep the soil moist, so there's no need to water. (You may need to water the soil once at the time of sowing in order for the water to be absorbed, but usually not.) After 14 days, it's time to harvest your microgreens!

CHEAP SEEDS TO MAKE MICROGREENS
→ dried yellow peas (1 kg/2¼ lb bag)
→ popcorn in a bag (not microwave popcorn)
→ sunflower seeds for birds

Yellow peas are particularly great. They will reshoot after the first harvest, sometimes even a third time. That bag of peas will really pay off!

Winter

Make the Most of Your Radiant Heat at Home

→ Some seeds, such as chillies and cucumbers, want their toes extra warm when they germinate. You can help them along with a little radiant heat from below. There are, of course, heat mats you can buy, but maybe you already have an extra-warm spot in your home? It's not my partner's favourite, though – she thinks the bathroom is for showering, not raising plants. But we all know I'm right.

YOU WILL NEED

→ seeds
→ tray
→ floor heating, boiler, radiator or heat mat

STEP BY STEP

1. Place the seeds on a tray and place the tray over a heat source. Aim for the temperature of the heat source to be 20–25°C (68–77°F).

2. Once the seeds have germinated, the heat is no longer so important. Then they will need light instead, so it's a good idea to move them to a window. (See page 160 on maximising light.)

Catch the Sunlight with a Tinfoil Mirror

→ Towards February in the northern hemisphere, the hours of sunlight begin to increase and soon it's time to start using your windows. If you want to get your propagation going a little earlier and prevent the plants from leaning or becoming too gangly, you can make a mirror out of tinfoil. That way, the sunlight from outside is reflected to make for more light on the plant – and from two directions. This will help your small plants grow plumper, and they won't lean outwards as much. If you want to take it to the next level, you can buy a space blanket (available in pharmacies). It can be hung as a curtain across the entire window or wherever you keep grow lights to make the most of the available light. It may not be the most popular decoration choice, but the plants love it!

YOU WILL NEED

→ scissors
→ a piece of cardboard, about 50 cm (20 inches) × the width of the window
→ tinfoil, enough to cover the cardboard
→ silver tape

STEP BY STEP

1. Cut the cardboard to cover the entire width of the window.
2. Wrap the cardboard surface in tinfoil and secure it with silver tape along the edges.
3. Put the tinfoil mirror in the window behind your pots and let the sun work its magic!

Fertiliser from Food Scraps

→ In winter, it can be difficult to make nettle tea or get hold of worm castings. However, it's easy to make your own fertiliser from food scraps you have at home. It will contain the necessary micro- and macronutrients, although the proportions between them are more precise in shop-bought liquid fertiliser. But it doesn't really matter! Most important are the macronutrients NPK – i.e. nitrogen, phosphorus and potassium – which you'll have in your fertiliser. Bananas contain phosphorus and potassium (and also magnesium). Eggshells contain phosphorus and potassium (and also calcium). And coffee grounds contain nitrogen, phosphorus, potassium and magnesium. Generally speaking, nitrogen stimulates the growth of leaves and other green plant parts, while phosphorus and potassium promote the production of flowers, fruits and berries.

YOU WILL NEED
→ a banana peel
→ two eggshells
→ grounds from two cups of coffee
→ 200 ml (7 fl oz) water
→ blender
→ glass jar with a lid

STEP BY STEP
1. Put the banana peel, eggshells, coffee grounds and water into the blender and blend thoroughly.
2. Pour the mixture into the glass jar. The sealed jar can be stored at room temperature for a couple of weeks before it goes bad.
3. Dilute the nutrient mix when watering; 50 ml (1¾ fl oz) per litre (¼ gallon) of water is good. How often you need to water depends on the plant; see how they respond and adjust. If some eggshell or banana peel ends up in the pot, they can be mixed into the soil.

Tropical Humidity Tent

→ Tropical plants like high humidity, but many homes are too dry in winter. The advice is often to spray and shower the plants with water, but that moisture evaporates quickly. A humidity tent traps the moisture inside and provides the plant with a more even microclimate. Don't forget to make some air holes for ventilation!

YOU WILL NEED

→ plastic packaging or a plastic bag that fits around the plant
→ plant support sticks that are slightly longer than the height of the plant (optional)
→ scissors

STEP BY STEP

1. Pull the plastic bag over the plant. If the plant is delicate, put a few support sticks into the pot. Make sure that they extend a little higher than the plant to form a scaffolding for the plastic bag to rest on.
2. Cut air holes in the top corners of the bag (i.e. the bottom corners). Also make sure that the bag doesn't close around the pot at the bottom, as this will increase the risk of mould.
3. Water as usual.

Winter

Ketchup Bottle Humidifier

→ Plants, especially tropical ones, need a lot of moisture, but in the northern hemisphere it tends to be dry indoors in winter. Misting and plastic covers work well, but some people (i.e. my partner) don't like the way they look. If you don't either, this humidifier is an option! Find a glass ketchup bottle, fill it with water and hang it on a radiator. The water evaporates at a good rate and, if the humidifier is located right next to the plant, it will increase the moisture content of the air in that spot for a longer period of time.

YOU WILL NEED

→ steel wire, 20 cm (8 inches) long
→ an empty, clean glass bottle with a screw cap, such as a ketchup bottle
→ pliers
→ water

STEP BY STEP

1. Wrap the wire around the neck of the bottle, just below the thread. Twist and tighten the wire with the pliers so that it sits firmly and the bottle can hang from it.
2. Using the pliers, bend the end of the wire into a hook.
3. Fill the bottle with water and hang it on a radiator next to the plant.
4. The water will slowly evaporate over a long period of time. Refill the bottle when it's empty.

Drip Watering with Snowballs

→ Water that falls from the sky is far better than tap water, especially for plants that don't like lime. If it snows in winter, you can put snowballs in your pots. As they melt, the air becomes humid and the plant absorbs both nutrients and water from the snow. In other words, it kills two birds with one stone!

YOU WILL NEED
→ snowballs

STEP BY STEP
1. Go outside and make some snowballs.
2. Place a snowball or two in each pot – ensuring the snowballs aren't directly touching the plant stem – and let them melt slowly.

Winter

Use Your Tools for Measuring

→ When planting, making garden beds and digging, you often need to measure things. But there is never a tape measure around when you need it … If it's not soil depth for bulbs, it's the distance between seeds and seedlings or the width of a garden bed. Make sure you always have the right measurements with the help of a barbecue fork. Simply burn marks at useful distances on all your tools with handles.

YOU WILL NEED

→ tape measure
→ pencil
→ rake, shovel, broom or similar with a wooden handle
→ barbecue fork

STEP BY STEP

1. Use a tape measure to mark various distances on the handle, such as 5, 10, 20, 50 and 120 cm (2, 4, 8, 20 and 47 inches).
2. Heat up the barbecue fork.
3. Hold the handle in one hand and the barbecue fork in the other. Place one of the barbecue fork's tines against one of the marks on the handle and roll the handle against the fork to burn it in. Repeat for the rest of the markings.

Winter

Pallet Plant Stand

→ Wooden pallets make for good building materials and are often free. Here, I have turned one into a plant stand that holds many pots and can easily be moved around. It's a great way to save space and make your garden feel cosy. Make sure it faces south (in the northern hemisphere) or north (in the southern hemisphere) and the plants will be set up to thrive!

YOU WILL NEED

→ a wooden pallet
→ crowbar
→ screwdriver and 6 cm (2½ inches) long screws
→ pots, 12 cm (4½ inches) in diameter (both plastic and terracotta are fine)

STEP BY STEP

1. The pallet has one side with five planks and one with three. Using a crowbar, remove planks number two and four on the side that has five. Now you should have three planks left that are aligned with the three planks on the other side (see page 174). The planks you have removed will be turned into supports to make the pallet steady.

2. Place the pallet upright with one long side against the ground.

3. Align one of the two removed planks across the pallet so that it is flush with the short side and the pallet is centred; it should look like an upside-down T (see page 175). Make sure the pallet is in the centre of the plank and screw the plank in place. Repeat with the second plank on the opposite short side.

4. Place your pots in the spaces between the three 'floors'. Place the pallet in a sunny spot and enjoy your plant wall!

Winter

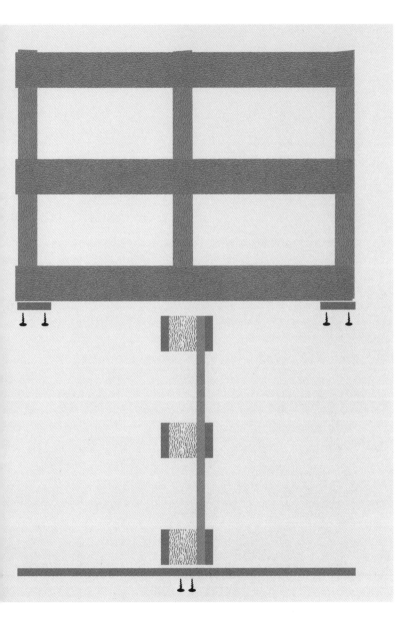

Winter

Pimp Your Raised Garden Bed

→ Raised garden beds are very popular, but they often look a bit dull. Some people paint the frame, but I like to spruce mine up by decorating with pieces of firewood all along the outside. This results in a more stable and robust garden bed as well as a stylish exterior. It also raises the edges a bit, so you can add more soil. If you wish, you can staple landscape fabric to the inside of the frame. It protects the soil from any residual chemicals in the frame and the wood from moisture, making it last longer.

YOU WILL NEED

→ a standard-size raised garden bed
→ about 50 pieces of firewood, 30 cm (12 inches) long
→ screwdriver and screws

STEP BY STEP

1. Place the raised garden bed frame on the ground.
2. Mount the logs on the outside of the frame, screwing them from the inside. Put one screw in the upper part of the logs and one in the lower part for better durability.
3. Place the logs closely together all the way around the frame. In spring, you can bring it outside, fill it with soil and start planting!

Herb Troughs

→ Using old gutters, you can make a customised plant arrangement that looks nice and takes up very little space. You can build your own ladder to hang them from, but one from the flea market looks best. By mounting the gutters at an angle and adding gravel for drainage, watering is a breeze!

YOU WILL NEED

→ screwdriver and screws
→ six gutter hooks
→ a ladder
→ drill and 25 mm (1 inch) drill bit
→ three gutters, 1 metre (3¼ feet) long
→ six gutter end caps
→ three pieces of insect netting, 10 × 10 cm (4 × 4 inches)
→ a few handfuls of gravel
→ three pieces of landscape fabric, 100 × 10 cm (3¼ feet x 4 inches)
→ soil

STEP BY STEP

1. Screw the hooks onto the ladder. Each section should be mounted at a slight angle so that water doesn't collect at the bottom. Therefore, don't make the hooks level. Instead, let one in each pair be slightly lower than the other. Alternate which side is higher, with a finished result that looks a bit like a Z leaning to the right, to allow water to flow from one level to the next.

2. Drill a hole about 5 cm (2 inches) in from the edge at one end of each gutter.

3. Attach the end caps to both ends of each gutter and fit the gutters into the hooks so that the ends with the holes are a little lower (this is where the water will flow out).

4. Put netting over the holes. Add 1 cm (½ inch) gravel to the bottom of each gutter for drainage. Cover with fabric, then add soil and start planting.

5. Water on the top section. Thanks to the slope and the holes, the surplus from each level will flow to the next!

ACKNOWLEDGEMENTS

Thanks to Hilding, Tina, Mikael and Henrik who helped develop the concept and idea. And to the rest of the GardenR team for all your help with the development of both the product and ideas: Myad, Ali, Philip, Einar, Lucas, Felix, My, Viktor and Jens.

1337Works and the Partner team for feedback and key insights: Mikael, Marcela, Tobias and Anders – and, of course, our trainees Axel, Vincent and Douglas.

The team at my Swedish publisher, Polaris Fakta, for doing a great job with the book: Petra, Karl, Hedvig, Sebastian and Cecilia.

Peter for fantastic photos!

My family for putting up with me and offering encouraging words and ideas: Pernilla, Ebba, Bosse, Birgitta and Bengt, Axel and Kristina, Rolf and Monika.

And especially to all my friends and followers for your generous comments and for cheering me on!

Finally, a big thanks to you for reading. I hope you have been inspired and enjoyed the book!

Index

Published in 2024 by Murdoch Books, an imprint of Allen & Unwin
First published as Trädgårdshacks in 2021 by Bokförlaget Polaris, Sweden
English edition published in agreement with Politiken Literary Agency and Bennet Agency

Murdoch Books UK
Ormond House
26–27 Boswell Street
London WC1N 3JZ
Phone: +44 (0) 20 8785 5995
murdochbooks.co.uk
info@murdochbooks.co.uk

Murdoch Books Australia
Cammeraygal Country
83 Alexander Street
Crows Nest NSW 2065
Phone: +61 (0)2 8425 0100
murdochbooks.com.au
info@murdochbooks.com.au

For corporate orders and custom publishing, contact our business development
team at salesenquiries@murdochbooks.com.au

Photography: Peter Carlsson
Designer: Sebastian Wadsted, Lyth & Co
Editor: Hedvig Ohlsson, Lyth & Co

Publisher: Céline Hughes
Translator: Alice Olsson
English-language editorial manager: Breanna Blundell
English-language editor: Kay Halsey
English-language cover designer: Sarah Odgers
Production director: Lou Playfair

Text and internal design © Filip Johansson and Bokförlaget Polaris 2021
The moral right of the author has been asserted.
Cover design © Sarah Odgers, Murdoch Books 2024
Photography © Peter Carlsson 2021, except for pages 15, 17, 18, 22, 36, 39, 43, 58, 61, 78, 95,
104, 108, 111, 120, 128, 132-133, 134, 137, 144, 153, 158, and 166 © Filip Johansson

*Murdoch Books acknowledges the Traditional Owners of the Country on which we live and
work. We pay our respects to all Aboriginal and Torres Strait Islander Elders, past and present.*

ISBN 978 1 76150 015 2

A catalogue record for this book is available from the British Library

A catalogue record for this
book is available from the
National Library of Australia

Printed by 1010 Printing International Limited, China

10 9 8 7 6 5 4 3 2 1

MIX
Paper | Supporting
responsible forestry
FSC® C016973